SYON

SYON HOUSE

River Thames

SYON PARK

INTRODUCTION
by His Grace The Duke of Northumberland

ESPERANCE EN DIEU

Welcome to Syon Park,

home to my family for over four hundred years, and still owned and looked after by us. Since the founding of Syon Abbey by King Henry V, Syon has had a turbulent time, as its occupants played on the centre stage of politics throughout its history. It is a wonderful home, full of beauty and magnificence, of great paintings and furniture, with perhaps the finest Robert Adam interior in the country. Surrounded by its own parkland, with Kew Gardens across the Thames, it is hard to believe that Syon is barely ten miles from central London.

As a child, with five brothers and sisters, I used to spend the summers at Syon, fishing in the lakes, playing tennis, swimming and playing on the hay bales in the meadow. Little has changed, and it is part of Syon's charm that fish still swim in the lakes, and cattle still graze the meadows. It is a haven for wildlife and with all the attractions available in the park, my wife and I hope your visit to Syon is a memorable experience.

Northumberland

The Site

Syon Park is a remarkable survival of a privately owned rural estate close to the centre of London. It is situated between the two great arterial routes of the Thames and the main road west from London.

Syon is a living landscape containing many elements of British history from prehistoric times to the present day. Its many changes reflect the wealth and power of its owners and have been expressed through the latest trends and technologies in architecture and design. Syon is now the only part of the tidal Thames with water meadows and a natural foreshore, and it is likely that much of the site once formed an island, or eyot, in the Thames. In prehistory the stretch of the river around Syon was a mass of creeks, islands and marshes, and it is likely that the line of the two lakes in the park represents a former channel or palaeochannel. Plentiful supplies of fish and game attracted early settlers to such islands and there is evidence of Neolithic, Bronze Age and Iron Age activities in the area with the foreshore in front of Syon House producing a wealth of archaeological finds from metal objects to fish traps.

A view of Brentford and the Thames foreshore during the Roman period. The site now occupied by Syon Park is on the bottom left of the picture.

Painting by G. Manchester from '2000 years of Brentford' by Roy Canham, London 1978.

Photo from 'Antiquities of Middlesex' by Montagu Sharpe, G. Bell 1919.

These stakes were found on the foreshore near Brentford Dock during the early 1900s and were probably associated with an Iron Age or Roman settlement on the river. A claim was made at the time that they formed part of the British defences against Caesar.

The islands would have provided opportunities for fording the river, and it was near Syon that the Romans possibly crossed the Thames in 54 BC. Later, there were Roman and Saxon settlements at Brentford, where the River Brent was forded by the main Roman road running west from London. In 1016 the Saxon King, Edmund Ironside, defeated the Danes led by Canute at the Battle of Brentford. Brentford, although not mentioned in the Domesday Book, was a thriving riverside community by the 14th century. To the south-west, Isleworth (*Gistelesworde*) was recorded in the Domesday Book and during the 13th century Richard of Cornwall owned a manor house in the village.

In 1415, King Henry V founded two religious houses, one dedicated to the Carthusian Order at Shene, on the opposite side of the river to Isleworth, and the other to the '*Order of St Saviour, the Blessed Virgin Mary and St Bridget of Syon*' at Twickenham. The endowment was a fulfilment of his father's penance for the part he played in the death of King Richard II. The Twickenham site proved unsuitable and the abbey was moved to the site now occupied by Syon House. Construction commenced in 1426 and by 1431 the first buildings were ready for occupation. The Bridgettine Order had been founded in the 14th century by the Swedish mystic, St Bridget, who established a monastery at Vadsterna. Syon (*Sion*) Park is named after the abbey and the abbey in turn takes its name from Mount Zion in the Holy Land.

Background image: Archaeological finds from 'Old England, Brentford' by R E M Wheeler, Antiquity 1929.

Syon House and its surroundings at the beginning of the 18th century painted by Jan Griffier.

Syon Abbey
(1415 – 1539)

Syon Abbey was the only Bridgettine house in England in the 15th century. The Order was unusual in that it accommodated separate communities of men and women, each requiring entirely independent quarters for living and prayer.

The abbey consisted of 60 sisters in one community and 13 priests, 4 deacons and 8 lay brothers in the other. The Abbess ruled both communities in all temporal affairs and the Confessor-General, the elected Superior of the Brothers, was responsible for spiritual direction.

No plans survive of the abbey buildings or their layout. Similar Bridgettine foundations were based on an inner cloister for the nuns, and an open, outer cloister for the brethren. The quadrangular shape of Syon House, with its central courtyard has given rise to the theory that it may have formed the nun's cloister. The only likely visible evidence of the abbey is a vaulted undercroft below the Great Hall. The location of the church, consecrated in

1488 remains a mystery, but if it followed a traditional Bridgettine form it would have been approximately one hundred metres in length, constructed of stone with plain glass windows. A geophysical survey has revealed possible lines of foundations. It must be

The Lady Abbess of Syon Abbey, South Brent, Devon with the iron cross and the pinnacle from the original abbey gateway at Syon.

assumed that the abbey buildings lie below the present house and lawns, and that the precinct extended into the area now occupied by the Garden Centre. The abbey was a large community, mainly self-sufficient in food with 30 acres of orchard and gardens.

Syon Abbey was at the time of its suppression in 1539 the tenth wealthiest in England. It was endowed with estates as far afield as St Michael's Mount in Cornwall and the *'messuage, land, meadow, wood, pasture and rent in Istelworth, Twykenham, Worton and Heston, with their appurtenances aforesaid, in free and perpetual alms for ever'*. Syon Abbey became renowned for its spiritual learning, public preaching and an extensive library of over 1,400 books and manuscripts. Such a wealthy and influential institution inevitably became embroiled in the religious turmoil of the reign of King Henry VIII. Queen Catherine of Aragon had been a regular visitor and in 1534 the abbey became connected with Elizabeth Barton *'the Holy Maid of Kent'*. She had particularly angered King Henry VIII by her visions which caused her to denounce his divorce from Queen Catherine. Meetings were arranged at Syon between Barton and Sir Thomas More, by the abbey's Confessor-General, Richard Reynolds. Conflict between the abbey and the Crown grew, and Government agents intent on suppressing the abbey made an exaggerated report *'certefying the Incontynensye of the Nunnes of Syon with the Friores'*. Richard Reynolds also refused to acknowledge the King's supremacy and in 1535 he was brutally executed along with three Carthusian priests and John Hale, the vicar of Isleworth. Reynold's body is said to have been placed on the abbey gateway, and he was later canonised as a martyr.

The Visitation and surrender of Syon Nunnery to the Commissioners, 1539 by Paul Falconer Poole (1807-79).
Courtesy of City of Bristol Museum & Art Gallery/Bridgeman Art Library

At the time of its suppression in 1539, the abbey had a community of 73 members. In 1557, the nuns were recalled by Queen Mary to re-establish themselves at Syon, but this restoration was short lived and, they left the country once more on the accession of Queen Elizabeth I, finally settling in Portugal in 1594. There they stayed until 1861 when they returned to England and settled in Devon. Today, they are the only community of religious women that has been in existence since the mid-16th century, and it is said that Abbess Jordan never surrendered the keys or common seal of Syon at the Suppression. When the 2nd Duke of Northumberland visited the Order in Lisbon, the Lady Abbess of the time remarked that she still had the keys of Syon House, to which the Duke replied 'Indeed Madam? But I have altered the locks since then'.

DAILY LIFE AT SYON ABBEY

The most important element of daily life was the prayer of what is called the Divine Office, celebrated seven times a day. Although the two communities at Syon were strictly segregated, they came together at these times to praise God, the Brothers behind the High Altar and the Sisters above the Nave.

The day started at about 5am, when the Brothers assembled in the church to sing Matins and Lauds, the Sisters following on in their choir. Masses would be celebrated and further Offices sung, after which at about 9.30am there was time for a 'collation', probably bread and water; a more substantial breakfast was provided for the sick, the elderly, the young and for those engaged in heavy work.

Following the next Office (Sext), High Mass was held for everyone physically able to attend. After the mid-day prayers the two communities would proceed to their respective refectories for dinner, the main meal of the day. It was the duty of the Cellaress to provide food and drink for everyone 'sick and whole', and each day she was to order meat, fish and vegetables 'as far as the market and purse will stretch'. After dinner, Grace was said in church.

During the afternoon, there was time for study, needlework or manual work, when the Sisters and, presumably the Brothers too, were allowed to speak until Evensong. Silence was strictly kept in the church choir, refectory, cloister and dormitory and always in the washing house. Signs were used wherever possible but it was permissible to speak in a whisper if really necessary.

At about 5pm, the Brothers would gather in the church for Evensong, the Sisters again following on. Shortly after supper, bells would call the Sisters to 'spiritual collation' in the Chapter House, where announcements would be made and a reading given from a holy book. During this time, the Brothers sang Compline. When their reading was over, the Sisters, too, sang Compline in their Choir.

This was the last communal prayer of the day: a Blessing with Holy Water was given, and everyone then retired to the dormitories at around 8.30pm. Silence was strictly observed until after Lady Mass the following morning.

Background image: Abbess Jordan from Aungier's 'History of Syon Monastery, Isleworth & Hounslow'.

The Tudors & Syon

*After the suppression of the abbey
in 1539, the estate became Crown
property. Catherine Howard, fifth wife
of King Henry VIII was confined at
Syon where she was allocated two
rooms 'furnished moderately as her life
and condition hath deserved', before
her execution in 1542.*

In 1547, the Duke of Somerset, the Lord Protector to the
young King Edward VI, took possession of the estate. He is
credited with starting the construction of the present house
in the Renaissance style, from the buildings of the abbey. In
addition with the help of his physician, the botanist William
Turner, he laid out what has been called the first botanic
garden in Britain, a grand formal garden in the latest Italian
style. In later years, Turner recalled meeting the young
Princess Elizabeth at Syon, and conversing with her in
Latin, which she spoke better than any woman he had met
on all his travels. It was also at Syon that Turner wrote his

The Lord Protector Somerset

1548 book '*The Names
of Herbes*'. Italian
gardens were essentially
an extension of
architecture into the
landscape and relied on
evergreens to provide
regular geometric
forms. This garden
would probably have
been based on avenues and terraces. However, Tudor
politics was full of dangers and there is an unsubstantiated
story that Somerset's political enemies, seeing the unfamiliar
form of the terraces and walks of the new Italian garden,

accused him of trying to fortify Syon. Somerset was accused
of plotting against the Crown and executed in 1552.

Syon was then acquired by one of his rivals, John Dudley,
Duke of Northumberland. The Duke's son, Lord Guildford
Dudley, had married Lady Jane
Grey, great-granddaughter of
King Henry VII, and it was
at Syon in 1553 that she
was formally offered the
Crown by the Duke.
She accepted reluctantly,
was conveyed to London
by river and proclaimed
Queen. Nine days later she was
displaced by Mary Tudor, and the
following year she was executed.

*Portrait of a lady thought
to be Lady Jane Grey, but
also considered to be
Princess Elizabeth.*

Syon reverted to Crown property in 1558 and while it is
not known when work on the house was completed, an
inventory of 1593 describes a substantial Tudor house
which could accommodate the Queen and her Court.
It is recorded that Queen Elizabeth made four visits to
Syon between 1576-1594.

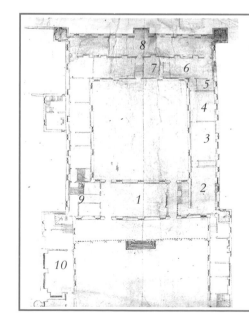

*The earliest known
plan of the house with
room layout based on a
1593 inventory.*

1. Hall
2. Great Chamber
3. Presence Chamber
4. Privy Chamber
5. Withdrawing
   Chamber
6. Bedchamber
7. Coffer Chamber
8. Long Gallery
9. Buttery & Pantry
10. Kitchens

When King Henry VIII died in 1547 his coffin lay for the night in the abbey church on its way from Westminster to Windsor. A curious prophecy was then fulfilled. In 1535, a Franciscan friar, named William Peto, when preaching before King Henry VIII, had declared ' that God's judgements were ready to fall upon his head ... and that the dogs would lick his blood as they had done Ahab's' ... Peto's prediction came true, when the following morning at Syon, a dog was found licking up certain remains which had managed to seep through the coffin from the bloated corpse inside. This was regarded as a divine judgement upon the King for his desecration of the abbey.

Detail from 'The Reward of Cruelty' by William Hogarth. Courtesy of the Wellcome Foundation.

HENRY, 9TH EARL

THOMAS, 7TH EARL

JOSCELINE, 11TH EARL

ALGERNON, 10TH EARL

ELIZABETH PERCY

ELIZABETH, 11TH COUNTESS

SIR HENRY PERCY (HOTSPUR.) 1402.

HUGH PERCY AS A BOY

THE PERCY FAMILY
THE EARLS AND DUKES OF NORTHUMBERLAND

ALGERNON PERCY, 4TH DUKE

GEORGE, 5TH DUKE

HUGH & CHARLOTTE 3RD DUKE & DUCHESS

Hugh Smithson & Elizabeth Seymour, 1st Duke & Duchess

Hugh & Frances 2nd Duke & Duchess

Algernon Seymour, 7th Duke of Somerset

Alan Ian & Helen, 8th Duke & Duchess

Algernon Percy, 6th Duke

Hugh & Elizabeth, 10th Duke & Duchess

Ralph & Jane, The present Duke & Duchess

Henry George, 7th Duke

George, 9th Duke

Henry Percy, 11th Duke

The Percy Family

Henry, 9th Earl of Northumberland (1584-1632), the first Percy to possess Syon, took great pride in his ancestors. He had compiled a great pedigree which traced his ancestry back to the Emperor Charlemagne.

One of his ancestors Sir Henry Percy (nicknamed Harry "Hotspur") who died at the Battle of Shrewsbury in 1403, was to be immortalised by Shakespeare during the Earl's lifetime.

William de Percy (d.1096), founder of this family, came to England at the time of the Norman Conquest. During the following three centuries the Percys established great estates north and south, principally in Sussex, Yorkshire, Lincolnshire, Cumberland and Northumberland. By the late 14th century, in Hotspur's time, they were at the height of their powers making and breaking kings. Thereafter through the civil conflicts of the 15th century and the political and religious twists of the 16th century, the line experienced deaths on the battlefield, executions at the block, dispossessions through attainder and murder in the Tower of London. Its resilience however, was such that two centuries of adversity and one long bout of princely living by the 'magnificent' 5th Earl failed to destroy the family.

Henry, the 9th Earl's extraordinary life followed the course of a true Renaissance nobleman, despite his deafness and 15 years as a prisoner.

The Earl had a love of learning and books, getting the scholars such as Thomas Harriot and William Warner to purchase volumes for him, buying others himself in the Low Countries and even having them imported from Spain. Like many lively and enquiring minds of his time, he was drawn to alchemy, hence his nickname of the 'Wizard Earl'.

There was a strong element of the Elizabethan adventurer in him. He took his band of military retainers on at least two expeditions to the wars in the Low Countries. Syon was the location for the Earl's armoury where he kept 100 muskets and 50 pistols. On an early expedition he became fashionable by having his ear pierced with a ring. He was interested in the New World and consumed with friends, such as Sir Walter Raleigh, great quantities of tobacco, and had potatoes on his household menu.

HENRY, 9TH EARL
(1584-1632)

The early 17th century archway named after the 9th Earl which today stands within the area occupied by the Garden Centre.

In 1594, the Earl, acquired Syon through his marriage to Dorothy Devereux, widow of Sir Thomas Perrot who had held Syon from the Crown.

The death of Queen Elizabeth in 1603 transformed the Earl's fortunes. His support of King James I brought even greater influence and wealth and he entertained the King to a sumptuous dinner at Syon. He was gifted the freehold of the Syon estate in 1604. However, from this high point

the Earl's fortunes were to change dramatically. A distant cousin, Thomas Percy, was the constable of the Earl's castle at Alnwick and had responsibility for administering the castle and its estates, as well as acting as his messenger to the Scottish court. Thomas was a staunch Catholic and one of the 'Gentlemen Pensioners' of whom the Earl was captain. On November 4th 1605, Thomas dined with the Earl at Syon and the next day the plot to blow up the Houses of Parliament was discovered. Thomas Percy was one of the principal Gunpowder Plotters and was shot dead making his escape in the Midlands.

One of the two 'Pepperpot' lodges built by the 9th Earl remain a distinctive feature of the approach to the house.

Two contemporary engravings describing Thomas Percy's involvement with the Gunpowder Plot of 1605. Below, Thomas is seen fifth from left, with Guido (Guy) Fawkes to the right. Below right, an engraving with vignettes describing his capture and death.

Courtesy of The National Portrait Gallery

The Martin Tower in the Tower of London where the 9th Earl was imprisoned.

carried out significant improvements to both the house and grounds at Syon, even during his imprisonment. A Mr Styckles was introduced "to give direction for garden work" and a new walled garden was laid out. It contained rose-trees and a variety of fruit trees, notably cherry, apricot, mulberry and quince. The gardener Anthony Menvell also brought herbs from Petworth. Other additions included a grapehouse, orchard and the attractively named "nightingale garden". On his release from the Tower in 1621, the Earl was confined to his estate at Petworth, where he died on November 5th 1632.

The Earl was immediately implicated through his association with Thomas and the fateful meeting at Syon. Though pleading his innocence, he was arrested, fined a massive £30,000, nearly £4 million in today's money, and kept in the Tower of London for 15 years. There he occupied the Martin Tower in some style. The accounts reveal that he kept twenty servants as well as being attended to by a barber and a corn cutter! New clothes were bought and copious quantities of wine and tobacco were consumed during his imprisonment. More than £200 was spent on wine and almost £50 on tobacco in one year. He created a laboratory and library, with books brought from Syon, and skeletons supplied by his physician, as well as 'retorts, crucibles, alembics, zodiacal charts and globes'. For recreation he made a pathway, thereafter known as '*Northumberland's Walk*' and busied himself with laying out gardens within the Tower, duly tended by a gardener from Syon. He built a bowling alley as well as becoming an expert at shove-halfpenny! The Earl was renowned in the Tower for his experiments in distilling alcohol, and, with deliveries of fruit from Syon, captivity was perhaps not excessively arduous. He was also able to re-acquaint himself with Sir Walter Raleigh, a fellow prisoner. The Earl

Thomas Harriot was the greatest English mathematician and astronomer of the period. He had been a long-time acquaintance of Sir Walter Raleigh, through whose influence he had become a pensioner of the 9th Earl. When the Earl was imprisoned, he gave Harriot use of the laboratory and a sleeping apartment in the Martin Tower. He then moved to a house at Syon, probably on the site of the present garages adjoining the house. At Syon on July 26th 1609 at 9am, he became the first European before Galileo to map the moon, made from observations through a crude telescope. He also went on to make notable observations such as the satellites surrounding Jupiter and sunspots.

Harriot's image of the moon from Petworth House Archives HMC 241/9, courtesy of Lord Egremont.

ALGERNON, 10th EARL
(1632-1668)

The 10th Earl's life was founded on a most unusual education, with his father building a schoolroom at the Tower, where he was instructed by William Warner. Books for study were brought from Syon, and the young Algernon lodged in Tower Hill where he kept a pet fox! Algernon inherited from his father a great love of learning and of fine art, second only to his monarch, King Charles I. He patronised the foremost artists of the day, principally Anthony Van Dyck and Peter Lely, and assembled an impressive collection of old masters. The fruits of his commissions and acquisitions can be seen today in the collections at Syon, Alnwick and Petworth.

Lord High Admiral and President of the Council of War under King Charles I, Algernon held back from full commitment to the Royalist cause and so lost his commands. Yet the war came close to home in 1642 when Syon House was damaged during the Battle of Brentford. This took place on 12th November 1642, when the king's army marched on London and attacked Parliamentarian forces stationed in the town. Prince Rupert made Syon House his headquarters during the battle, and there was a heated exchange of fire with several ships and barges on the river. As a result repairs had to be made to the house '*where it was shot through with ordnance*'. The Parliamentarian forces were outnumbered and retreated to the river where some were drowned and others, including John Lilburne, later to found the radical political movement known as the Levellers, were forced to surrender. The victorious Royalist troops ransacked the houses and taverns of Brentford – an act of brutality known as 'the Rape of Brentford'. The Royalist march on London was halted by the City of London Militia at Turnham Green.

Algernon supported a compromise between King and people which established his reputation for impartiality, and after the King was arrested and imprisoned he was made governor to James, Duke of York and the younger royal children from 1646-1649. King Charles I, when held at Hampton Court, was able to visit the children at Syon.

'*Syon House, August 23, 1647: His Majesty came hither to see his children this morning early, with one troop of Horse, and the Commissioners, and dined here. August 29, 1647 The King hunted in Richmond Park, and afterwards dined here with his children at Syon*'.

It may have been during one of these visits that Sir Peter Lely, painted the picture (shown below) of
King Charles I and the Duke of York,

which now hangs in the Red Drawing Room, for which he was paid £20.

Syon was a favourite spot for the Earl's own children who spent their summers there. The Earl kept Syon as a magnificent residence: 386 skins of leather hangings in the family colours of blue and gold clad the new staircase constructed in 1636; all 168 casements to the house's windows were painted; and in 1639 the wainscot in the gallery was gilded.

His interest in horticulture is shown by his participation in the great tulip speculation known as 'Tulipmania', spending the huge sum of £21 on imported bulbs. Indeed, this must have been among his earliest actions on succeeding to the title, as the market crashed in 1634, only two years after the death of the 9th Earl.

Syon House in the early 17th century. Built of Dunstable stone it was referred to as the 'white house'.

By the early 17th century, the lead in garden design had moved from Italy to France, and Algernon employed a French gardener to lay out a new garden to the south of Syon House, centred on a Great Fountain. The French gardens of the time were very formal, and the new garden at Syon was one of the first examples of this style in the country, with parterres and allées of lime and cypress.

The house was used for a Council meeting by Cromwell in 1647 and also in 1665 by King Charles II, when the Plague was raging in London. The writer John Evelyn commented '*when business was over I viewed that seat of the Earl of Northumberland, built out of an old Nunnery of stone and fair enough, but more celebrated for its garden than it deserves, yet there is excellent wall fruite and a pretty fountain, nothing else extraordinary*'. The 10th Earl retired to Syon and carried on developing the gardens, introducing many new and rare plants, as well as continuing to develop the orchards and kitchen gardens. There are records of artichokes, asparagus, melons and strawberries, as well as grapes, cherries, and more humble produce.

The Seymours

The Percys emerged in the Restoration period with their vast estates intact, until the death of the young 11th Earl, Josceline (1668-1670) left an infant daughter, Elizabeth, as his sole heir.

Elizabeth Percy had to face numerous ordeals, despite her wealth and the seeming independence of her own household. There was dispute over her guardianship in which her grandmother, Elizabeth Howard, second wife and widow of the 10th Earl, triumphed over her mother, Elizabeth Wriothesley, widow of Josceline. Since Elizabeth was a most eligible young heiress, her grandmother was busy from the time the girl reached the age of 12 brokering a suitable marriage. There were three marriages contracted within three years between 1679 and 1682: first to Henry, Earl of Ogle, who died within six months, then to Thomas Thynne, from whom Elizabeth fled abroad and who was later murdered; and finally to the young Charles Seymour, the 6th Duke of Somerset, who became known as the '*Proud Duke*'.

Elizabeth was an intimate of Princess Anne. When Anne quarrelled with her sister Queen Mary, who objected to her friendship with the Duchess of Marlborough, the Duke and Duchess placed Syon at her disposal. The princess gave birth to a son George, while she was in residence in 1692, but he died within hours.

The 6th Duke and Duchess of Somerset were prominent courtiers and held a series of influential posts. When Anne became Queen, the Duchess was appointed her Mistress of the Stole and Charles Seymour was Master of the Horse. His interests were widespread: he restored Petworth House, bought paintings and silverware, patronised artists, especially Michael Dahl, and enjoyed racing at Newmarket.

The Duke was particularly fond of horses and Syon became the principal stables where he would change horses when travelling between Petworth and London. It was often there that he met his Duchess, and she even travelled to Syon to meet him just days before her death in 1722. Primarily a summer residence, Syon would be prepared for them in advance, with servants arriving by barge to install gilt leather and damask hangings, paintings, curtains and beds.

Partly inspired by the writings of John Evelyn, avenues had become highly fashionable, and one of the great works of this period was the planting of a series of avenues of lime

The painting of Petworth House, West Sussex in the late 17th century, has been attributed to Jan Griffier. This view pre-dates the great re-modelling of the house undertaken by the 6th Duke of Somerset and the landscaping of the park by 'Capability' Brown in the 1750s.

trees. Several individual trees remain of the avenue running towards Isleworth, but the chief example is the great Lime Avenue to the west of Syon House. By creating the Avenue as a grand entrance drive, Somerset effectively increased the extent of the grounds surrounding the house, thus enhancing his prestige. This re-alignment towards the road also signalled that improvements to the roads were beginning to reduce the importance of the river as a means of transport.

View of Lime Avenue from Syon House.

In 1715, the Duke's son and heir Algernon, who had enjoyed a military career and was adjutant to the Duke of Marlborough, married Frances Thynne of Longleat, a *'blue stocking'* of her age and a patroness of poets and hymn-writers. She was profoundly disliked by her father-in-law, and it was the death in 1744 of their only son George, Lord Beauchamp, while on Grand Tour in Italy, that provoked a family crisis. The 6th Duke sought to use this occasion of tragedy to disinherit Algernon's surviving child, Elizabeth, so as to favour his other grandsons, the children of Sir William Wyndham.

Algernon, however, fought back against the disinheritance of his daughter, taking his cause personally to King George II who judged that the great Northumberland estates must remain with Algernon's issue along with Northumberland House and Syon. Wyndham, however, succeeded on Algernon's death to vast lands in Sussex, Yorkshire and Cumberland.

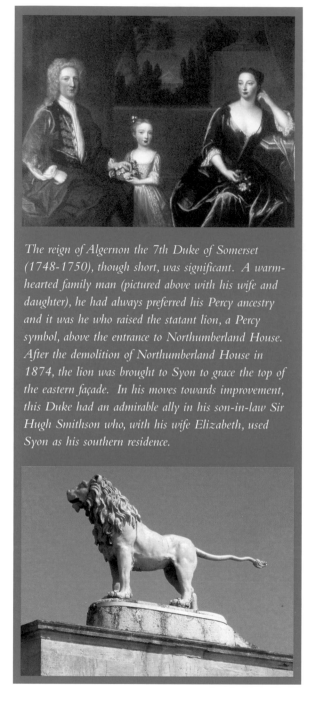

The reign of Algernon the 7th Duke of Somerset (1748-1750), though short, was significant. A warm-hearted family man (pictured above with his wife and daughter), he had always preferred his Percy ancestry and it was he who raised the statant lion, a Percy symbol, above the entrance to Northumberland House. After the demolition of Northumberland House in 1874, the lion was brought to Syon to grace the top of the eastern façade. In his moves towards improvement, this Duke had an admirable ally in his son-in-law Sir Hugh Smithson who, with his wife Elizabeth, used Syon as his southern residence.

The lives of Elizabeth Seymour and her husband Sir Hugh Smithson had been transformed by the death of her brother in 1744. Unusually for the age, theirs was a love match, and when they married in 1740 their future seemed destined to be that of a prosperous Yorkshire country squire and his wife. They lived at Stanwick, near Richmond, where he managed his estates and attended Parliament, while she concerned herself with running a provincial household.

The 1st Duke and Duchess of Northumberland

The Duke brought tried experience, mature judgement and an acute and enquiring mind to his task of modernising the Percy lands and properties. Even as a courtier his great interest in science was acknowledged and if the chimneys of Kensington Palace smoked, it was his advice that was sought!

He transformed and modernised the administration of his estates, enclosed and planted woodlands, and exploited the industrial potential of his lands, particularly coal mining. He invested income from improved rents in the restoration of the principal Percy seats: Northumberland House, Alnwick Castle and Syon House.

Elizabeth, 1st Duchess, was very proud of her Percy ancestry and totally committed to her husband's schemes, keeping an eye on the restoration work at Syon, which she reported to her husband in her letters. She liked to travel from London to Syon by state barge, being serenaded on the way by musicians. A great collector and commentator, she left a fascinating record of her life and times in her diaries.

Sir Hugh Smithson inherited the Percy estates and the title of Earl of Northumberland in 1750 and reigned as Earl and Duke (created 1766) of Northumberland until 1786. His marriage, title and vast inheritance thrust him to the forefront of the nobility and the nation's affairs.

The Duke and Duchess were determined to make their mark on Syon, but the house was somewhat dilapidated and the grounds had never recovered from an excessively hard frost in 1739, which killed many trees, robbing the formal grounds of much of their structure. The solution was a complete redesign of the estate, with the Scottish architect, Robert Adam being instructed to remodel the interior of the house and the Northumbrian designer, Lancelot '*Capability*' Brown, being called upon to lay out the grounds in the fashionable style of the English Landscape Movement. Brown and Adam had more in common than just being the fashionable designers of their day, both were aspiring to create a new, ideal form of an earlier time.

Thus while Adam's architecture was inspired by Classical Rome, so Brown took the mediaeval deer park as a model for an ideal countryside. Both were consciously borrowing the connotations of wealth, power and antiquity, and packaging them for their clients.

The Duke was one of Robert Adam's chief patrons and engaged him soon after Adam returned from Italy. In 1761, Adam published his plan for the interior decoration of Syon House. This included a design for a complete suite of rooms on the principal level, together with a rotunda to be erected in the main courtyard. In the event, five main rooms on the west, south and east sides of the house, stretching from the hall to the gallery, were refurbished in a classical style. It was enough to place a stamp on the architect and his work and it has been said that 'at Syon the Adam style was actually initiated'.

Adam's plans were put into execution by a team of craftsmen and artists, including the stuccoist Joseph Rose, the sculptors Joseph Wilton and John Cheere, the decorative artists Michelangelo Pergolesi and Pietro Cipriani and the figurative artists Francesco Zuccarelli and Andrea Casali. Antique statuary was imported from Rome by Adam's brother James, as were the scagliola columns and the three great bronze statues by Luigi Valadier.

The works inside the house were mirrored in the grounds and Syon was described as 'one of the finest villas in Europe'. Brown was the most influential figure of the landscape movement, which reacted to the formality of the French tradition. He created integrated landscapes that enhanced rather than controlled. While in many ways as artificial as the formal landscapes they replaced, Brown's works looked natural, as if they had been there for many years.

Brown extended the park into surrounding farmland, diverting the old road from Isleworth to Brentford, demolished various farm buildings and, taking advantage of the damp fields along the line of the prehistoric channel of the Thames, excavated two new lakes. Trees were essential to Brown's style, and suitably sited specimens and clumps, including some that are still standing, were retained. In addition, in 1764, George III commissioned Brown to landscape the grounds of his palace, on the site which is now Kew Gardens, with the river as the centrepiece rather than the dividing line. While Brown's work at Kew has long since been concealed by later developments, it was unique in the 18th century as the only example of adjacent Brown landscapes. Brown was also commissioned by Lord Holdernesse to landscape Sion Hill, a neighbouring property to the north.

The terraces and walks around the house were removed, and replaced by sweeping lawns and by the ha-ha, built largely by the local mason Thomas Hardwick, but the biggest change took place to the north of Syon House. Here the orchards and vegetable gardens were re-located to what is now the site of the Brent Lea estate. In their place Brown created 'Syon Pleasure Ground', centred on the Inner Lake, with trees and walks, boasting 'every foreign shrub, plant and flower which may be adopted by the soil of this climate', and 'the choicest trees and plants from all quarters of the globe' as well as a statue of the goddess Flora on a 55 foot Doric column. This changed the orientation of Syon Park, with the ornamental grounds relocated from the south and east to the north and west. The new 'productive' gardens also gave an opportunity to increase the range of crops grown: a hot wall was built for the growing of vines, new melon pits were dug, and stove houses built for the cultivation of pineapples. It would have been in one of these buildings that the first tea plant to grow in Europe flowered in 1773.

Background image: Robert Adam's plan for Syon which was never completed. The rotunda in the Courtyard was intended for entertaining.

Hugh, the 2nd Duke (1786-1817), made the army his career. As a lad of 16, he raised a company of recruits from Alnwick to serve in the army with him in the Seven Years War (1756-1763). He served with distinction as a general in the War of American Independence, commanding the relief force at Lexington. At Syon, the 2nd Duke consolidated the restoration work of his father. James Wyatt built the stable block, including the coach house to the north west of the house and the bridge over the outer lake at the west end of the Lime Avenue. The Duke also continued the development of the plant collection. American plants were fashionable at this time, and it is likely that the records of American introductions from this date refer to plants the Duke may have seen while on active service. Many of these would have been planted in the new area of Wilderness Garden, which was now extended as far as Isleworth, where a menagerie had been built in 1760. Golden pheasants were sent from Longleat in 1773 to join swans, geese, guinea fowl and ducks, and even a bear, with its own attendant servant. In 1803, close by the menagerie, the architect Robert Mylne began work on a pavilion with an adjoining boat house for the state barge.

During this period, the labour force in the gardens numbered between 14 and 16 gardeners. Head gardeners included James Meader, who wrote *The Planter's Guide* in 1779 before going on to Russia where he served Catherine the Great in her '*English*' Garden at Tsarskoe Selo, and William Forsyth who became a royal gardener. During most of his reign, the 2nd Duke was served by Thomas Hoy, who is buried in the graveyard of Isleworth Parish Church. The plants Forsythia and Hoya were named in honour of these last two gardeners.

The children of the 2nd Duke of Northumberland in the gardens at Syon.

The inheritance which the 2nd Duke left to his eldest son and successor **Hugh, 3rd Duke (1817-1847)**, made him the richest commoner in Britain, with huge royalties from wayleaves and from the coal mines of the north-east, as well as an immense estate rental.

A courtier, who inherited his father's loyalty to the Prince Regent, the Duke was rewarded by King George IV with the honour of being the King's personal representative at the coronation of King Charles X of France in 1825. It was an occasion which called for a display of dazzle and glitter which the Duke could comfortably undertake from his own immense wealth. Later, in 1829-1830, the same lavishness and display of patronage accompanied the Duke's Vice Regency of Ireland.

Hugh, 3rd Duke of Northumberland by Richard Dighton

The Great Conservatory, with the 19th century bronze statue of Mercury in the foreground,
a copy of the 16th century original by Giovanni da Bologna.

The power and influence of the Percys was confirmed when *Duchess Charlotte Florentia* was appointed as official governess to the young Princess Victoria. This role, which the Duchess fulfilled for more than 6 years (1831-1837), included overseeing the Princess's education and accompanying her on court occasions. The governess' function had been devised by the Princess' uncle, Prince Leopold of the Belgians and the Duchess at Syon. The room used by the young Victoria when she stayed with the Duchess at Syon is still called Princess Victoria's Room.

On Victoria becoming Queen, the Duke of Wellington wrote to the Duchess '*I have returned from the council at Kensington so delighted with your pupil that I can not deny myself the gratification of letting you know what an impression Her Majesty made on the Council at large.*'

The Duchess called Syon '*this delicious place*' , ranking it above all other residences. *The 3rd Duke* shared his Duchess' affection for Syon. The fabric of Syon house and park as seen today is testimony to this. The house was restored and provided with every amenity, the technologically innovative conservatory was built, and the gardens brought to a state of near horticultural perfection. The architect, Thomas Cundy, provided the chief entrance to the house with a porte-cochère, the north wing was extended, and the exterior was re-clad in Bath stone. Inside the house, the scagliola floor of the Ante Room was restored by William Croggan and the re-gilding of the interior ornament was carried out by Thomas Ponsonby. Robert Hughes was commissioned to supply new furnishings. The present day plan of the house reflects the additions and alterations carried out by the 3rd Duke.

This Duke was fascinated by gardening, and became a patron of influential writers such as John Claudius Loudon, who dedicated his *Arboretum et Fruticetum Britannicum* to him. The work includes numerous illustrations of trees growing at Syon, and Loudon acknowledged the encouragement the Duke had always given to gardening and '*more especially to the introduction and cultivation of foreign trees and shrubs.*' This interest in exotic plants led the Duke to rebuild the nursery and

kitchen grounds at Syon, and also to build what is now the centrepiece of the Gardens, the Great Conservatory.

The Great Conservatory was built between 1826 and 1827 to the rear of the old botanic house, which was sensibly preserved until the peach crop of 1827 had ripened. The masonry work was undertaken in Bath stone by Thomas Cundy, and the metalwork and furnaces by the garden engineering specialists James Richards of Birmingham. The architect of this remarkable building was Charles Fowler, co-founder of the Institute of British Architects and designer of the covered market at Covent Garden. At Syon Fowler also designed the Riding School with its iron truss roof and the clock tower on the stable block.

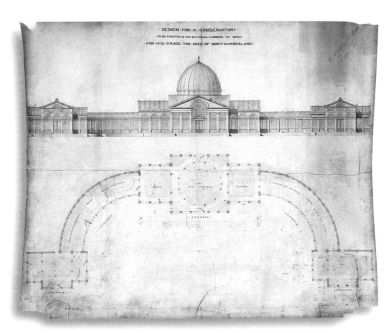

*'DESIGN FOR A CONSERVATORY
TO BE ERECTED IN THE BOTANICAL GARDENS AT SYON
FOR HIS GRACE THE DUKE OF NORTHUMBERLAND'*

What Fowler constructed in the gardens has been described as a conservatory in a transitional style, a cross between the 18th century orangery and a Victorian conservatory: the side wings are characteristic of the old-style orangery while the structure of the central building with its glass dome incorporated the latest technical advances in glasshouse design.

The inspiration for the layout of the conservatory was again classical, as Fowler turned to the works of Palladio and took as his model the unfinished villa of the Counts Lodovico and Francesco Trissino at Meledo. Instead of the dome over the central section of the villa, he applied the new theories of curvilinear greenhouses to create a glass dome surmounted by a cupola, which was as technologically advanced as it was architecturally innovative, with pillars and trusses constructed of cast iron but with the ribs of the dome made of wrought iron. This design of building permitted high levels of natural light, complemented by an elaborate and advanced heating system, with four miles of piping. Letters show that the Duke took a close interest in the smallest technical detail of the construction, and insisted on being kept informed of any changes or problems that occurred. With regard to planting, Fowler consulted with the head gardener and botanist Richard Forrest, and divided the building into a number of separate sections. From west to east, these held plants from the Cape and New Holland, the contemporary name for Australia, then heaths, which would have been representatives of the epacridaceae, fynbos plants from the tip of South Africa. There was a section for small stove (tropical) plants, before opening into the main dome which was planted as a tropical house with palms and giant bamboo in pots and planters. The east wing held a collection of African geraniums *(pelargoniums)*, before another section for heaths, and finally staging for camellias from India and China.

The plants grown in the Great Conservatory were often the latest discoveries from what was then the edge of the known world. The early 19th century was a time of great commercial and imperial expansion, and plants came to Syon by the box-load, from the Cape of Good Hope, West Africa, the West Indies, Australia, Mexico, South America, Ceylon, India, the Celebes, the Philippines and the South Seas. Despatches from the Botanical gardens at Calcutta included orchids from Nepal, pine seeds from the Himalayas, and the Duke even sent his own ship across the world to collect specimens. Richard Forrest published his *Alphabetical Catalogue of Plants of Syon Garden* in 1831, and listed over 3,000 species of trees and plants, of which 700 were hardy trees and shrubs, more than 1,000 hardy herbaceous plants, and over 1,500 glasshouse or tropical plants. Grape vines from Syon were sent out to Australia at this time, where they laid the foundations of the country's wine industry. Fifteen botanical gardeners worked in the Great Conservatory and the huge range of service glasshouses behind the scenes.

When **Algernon, 4th Duke (1847– 1865)** succeeded his brother, he was already a man of mature judgement and became known as '*Algernon the Good*'. His youth had been spent as a midshipman and naval officer in the Napoleonic Wars and later he served as First Lord of the Admiralty in Lord Derby's administration (1852). Politically enlightened his aim as a great land-owner was to provide well for his dependants and make his possessions an amenity for the wide community to enjoy. He opened up his parks and gardens, he sent his artisans and labourers to London to see the Great Exhibition of 1851, and in the summer of that year opened Syon House and Northumberland House to the public. When the giant waterlily *Victoria amazonica* was propagated at Syon for

Syon was used as a summer residence, renowned for the magnificent fêtes hosted in marquees on the lawns where after a sumptuous banquet there would be dancing and fireworks.

the first time in Britain, it was exhibited at the Great Exhibition and taken on a tour of different cities. During his reign, Giovanni Montiroli, the Italian architect who oversaw work at Alnwick Castle, was commissioned to design the ceilings in the Print Room, Green Drawing Room and Private Dining Room.

Throughout the 19th century Syon continued to be maintained as a rural aristocratic estate. The plant collections continued to flourish, and horticultural triumphs included the production of the first ripe mangosteens and coconuts to be produced in the country, as well as cloves, nutmeg, cocoa and vanilla. Flowers were grown at Syon to decorate the house and fruit was sent to Alnwick. A Syon gardener regularly travelled to London to tend the window boxes of the family's town house. The 4th Duke had purchased a 140 foot marquee for garden parties which was decorated with banks of blooms from the conservatory, and both social and charitable events were regularly held. By the end of the century, an article in Country Life recorded '*On every hand something will arrest attention. The trees are magnificent, ash, beech, elm and chestnut spreading their noble arms to cast shadows over the grass. Spacious lawns surround the house, and in the background on either side are bold sweeping shrubberies.....It is impossible to mention every valuable tree at Syon*'.

 **George, 5th Duke (1865–1867)**, first cousin of the 3rd and 4th Dukes, succeeded in 1865 at the great age of 87, and was followed on his death two years later by his son,

 Algernon, 6th Duke (1867–1899), who married Louisa, daughter and heiress of Henry Drummond, banker, political philosopher and religious reformer. The Duke and Duchess followed Drummond as prominent members of the Catholic Apostolic movement and inherited his Surrey estate and Albury Park, with its famous Evelyn gardens and church of the Catholic Apostolic sect.

 Both the 6th Duke and his son **Henry George, 7th Duke (1899–1918)** were courtiers and active politicians. During the First World War the Riding School was converted into hospital ward accommodation and the house was placed at the disposal of the British Red Cross Society.

The **8th Duke, Alan Ian (1918–1930)**, had spent a lifetime as a career soldier, and fought in the First World War. The social and political disruption resulting from the war  left its mark on Syon: the growth of London led to development along the Great West Road, and the park itself came under threat from a proposed sewage works. Large private estates were proving increasingly costly to run, but the fact that the family still used Syon as one of their principal residences meant that the estate survived the economic crises of the 1930s and continued to provide much-needed local employment. The burden of providing leadership to the family during the 8th Duke's illness and the 9th Duke's minority, thereafter fell to the remarkable Helen, 8th Duchess, a daughter of the Duke of

*Helen, 8th Duchess
of Northumberland
by Philip de Laszlo*

Richmond. She was an active promoter of the family's interest at both local and national level for more than half a century, from her marriage in 1911 to her death in 1965. She served HM Queen Elizabeth the Queen Mother for many years as Mistress of the Robes.

During the Second World War **George, the 9th Duke, (1930–1940)**, offered a wing of Syon House as accommodation for Guards officers, one of whom recalled: '*George Northumberland kindly opened a wing of his house at Sion. There we were to live in the greatest elegance - but in great discomfort from the intense cold.*' The Duke was killed in action in Northern France at the age of 29. During the war incendiary bombs caused damage to the park and house, and when the neighbouring West Middlesex Hospital was hit, Syon House was volunteered for nurses' accommodation.

The reign of the **10th Duke, Hugh (1940-1988)** saw the successful transformation of a great estate to meet the changing requirements of the second half of the 20th century. The Duke was recognised as a leading agriculturist of the day, whose deep interest in related sciences led him to chair the government investigation into bovine foot and mouth disease (1968) and the Medical Research Council. He served as Steward of the Royal Household. In 1946, the Duke married Elizabeth Montagu Douglas Scott, daughter of the Duke of Buccleuch; they had six children

Duke Hugh had a deep affection for Syon. After the war, he used Syon as his regular summer seat and opened the house for public viewing in 1951. The Great Conservatory became the focus of the gradual regeneration of the gardens and the Duke sought to finance this work through a National Garden Exhibition in partnership with ICI, culminating in 1968 with the opening of the Gardening

Centre Ltd. This included the conversion of the former Riding School and stable yard and the introduction of display gardens within the pleasure grounds. The exhibition closed in the early 1970s and in the subsequent years a number of commercial and visitor attractions were established in the park.

Henry, the 11th Duke, made Syon his permanent home during his reign (1988-1995). In 1994 the outer lake in the park was opened as a trout fishery. He died unmarried. His brother and successor **Ralph, the present 12th Duke**, is married to Jane Richard. They have four children.

Photo courtesy of Skyscan

THE PERCY FAMILY AT
SYON HOUSE

HENRY PERCY, K.G.
9th Earl of Northumberland,
b. 1564 d. 1632
(imprisoned in the Tower 1605 - 1622)

Dorothy, daughter of
Walter Devereux,
1st Earl of Essex
d. 1619

ALGERNON PERCY, K.G.
10th Earl of Northumberland,
b. 1602 d. 1668

Elizabeth, daughter of
Theophilus Howard,
2nd Earl of Suffolk
d. 1705

JOSCELINE PERCY
11th Earl of Northumberland,
b. 1644 d. 1670

Elizabeth, daughter of
Thomas Wriothesley,
4th Earl of Southampton
d. 1690

ELIZABETH PERCY
b. 1667 d. 1722

(1) Earl of Ogle
(2) Thomas Thynne
(3) Charles, 6th Duke of
     Somerset
     b. 1662 d. 1748

ALGERNON SEYMOUR
7th Duke of Somerset, b. 1684 d. 1750;
created Earl of Northumberland 1749
with remainder in default of male heirs
to his son-in-law

Frances, daughter of
Hon. Henry Thynne
d. 1754

ELIZABETH SEYMOUR
b. 1716 d. 1776

Sir Hugh Smithson, K.G. b. 1714/15 d. 1786
Succeeded as Earl of Northumberland 1750,
taking the names and arms of Percy; created
1st Duke of Northumberland 1766

HUGH PERCY K.G.
2nd Duke,
b. 1742 d. 1817

Frances, daughter of
Peter Burrell of
Beckenham, Kent
b. 1752 d. 1820

Algernon Percy
1st Earl of Beverley
b. 1750 d. 1830

Isabella, daughter of
Peter Burrell of
Beckenham, Kent
d. 1812

HUGH PERCY K.G.
3rd Duke,
b. 1785 d. 1847

Charlotte Florentia,
daughter of Edward
Clive, Earl of Powis
b. 1787 d. 1866

ALGERNON PERCY K.G.
4th Duke,
b. 1792 d. 1865

Eleanor, daughter of
Richard Grosvenor, 2nd
Marquess of Westminster
b. 1820 d. 1911

GEORGE PERCY
5th Duke, b. 1788 d. 1867

Louisa, daughter of
Hon. James Archibald
Stuart-Wortley Mackenzie
b. 1781 d. 1848

ALGERNON PERCY, K.G.
6th Duke, b. 1810 d. 1899

Louisa, daughter of
Henry Drummond of
Albury Park, Surrey
b. 1813 d. 1890

HENRY GEORGE PERCY, K.G.
7th Duke, b. 1846 d. 1918

Edith, daughter of
George Douglas Campbell
7th Duke of Argyll
b. 1849 d. 1913

ALAN IAN PERCY, K.G.
8th Duke, b. 1880 d. 1930

Helen, daughter of
Charles Gordon-Lennox
7th Duke of Richmond
b. 1886 d. 1965

HENRY GEORGE ALAN PERCY
9th Duke, b. 1912 d. 1940
(killed in action)

HUGH ALGERNON PERCY, K.G.
10th Duke, b. 1914 d. 1988

Elizabeth, daughter of
8th Duke of Buccleuch
b. 1922

HENRY ALAN WALTER RICHARD PERCY
11th Duke, b. 1953 d. 1995

RALPH GEORGE ALGERNON PERCY
12th Duke, b. 1956

Jane, daughter of
John Richard
b. 1958

The House

The Great Hall

*The entrance to the Great Hall is through the porte-cochère,
built in the 1820s, when the exterior walls of the house were resurfaced
with Bath stone by the 3rd Duke.*

The Great Hall is almost a double cube, measuring 66 feet (20.1 metres) by 31 feet (9.4 metres) by 34 feet (10.3 metres).

Based on a Roman Basilica and probably inspired by the work of Piranesi, it realises the full grandeur of Robert Adam's conception; work started on it in 1762 and finished in 1769.

Robert Adam (1728-1792).
Courtesy of the National Portrait Gallery, London

Adam's instructions were '*to create a palace of Graeco-Roman splendour*'. He was confronted with difficulties in the uneven floor levels of the Tudor house, the hall was above the outside ground levels but below the principal interior floor level. Adam was not allowed to alter those levels, the general layout of the rooms or the main structure of the house. He overcame these problems by the two-armed staircase leading to a tunnel-vaulted recess with a screen of Doric columns, supporting the entablature which continues around the hall. At the other end of the hall is a shallow step up to the coffered apse, and behind this the concealed steps leading to the rest of the house, hidden by curved doors. The apse and recess solved the problem of dimension as regards length, and the ceiling with its great beams is reflected in the pattern of the marble flooring.

Adam employed Joseph Rose to do the decorative stucco work. In its original state, the hall was decorated throughout in white, broken only by the black and white marble flooring. It was repainted in 1974 to a colour plan by John Fowler.

The four antique statues are standing on pedestals designed by Adam and executed by Joseph Rose. The statues are of *Livia*, mother of the Emperor Tiberius, *a lady of the third century AD*, *a Roman magistrate*, and *a Roman in a toga*.

The Hall is dominated at either end by the particularly fine statues of the *Dying Gaul* and the *Apollo Belvedere*. The *Dying Gaul* by Valadier, is a copy of the original in the Capitoline Museum in Rome. The bronze was cast in Rome and its colour achieved by immersion in water for nine years. Notes made in her own handwriting by the 1st Duchess of Northumberland in 1773 record that £300 was paid for the bronze. At the opposite end stands the *Apollo Belvedere*, a copy by John Cheere of the original in the Vatican which cost £21 in 1764. The original dates from about 280 B.C and was cast to honour Apollo, who, according to legend saved the Temple of Delphi from the Gallic army.

The antique classical busts include *Antisthenes*, *Socrates, the
Emperor Claudius* and *Marcus Aurelius*. There are also busts
of the *1st Duke of Northumberland* by Van Nost the younger
and *William Pitt the younger* by Nollekens.

The pier table positioned in front of the *Dying Gaul* was
designed by Adam. Its pinewood frame is overlaid with
gesso and the top has an inlay of coloured marble, with
typical anthemion design.

The chiaroscuro circular paintings are by Andrea Casali,
with details taken from the Triumphal
Arches of Rome.

*Marble bust
of Socrates.*

The Ante Room

The contrast between the Great Hall and the Ante Room or Vestibule is startling. Here the vivid colourings are enhanced by the twelve Ionic columns veneered with verd-antique scagliola, obtained by James Adam in Rome in 1765. The gilded statues above were executed by John Cheere.

The floor is a remarkable example of highly polished scagliola, which is a composition of marble, fixing materials and colouring matter. Wear to the original floor necessitated its relaying in 1832 by William Croggan, and careful examination will reveal that more recent restoration work has been carried out. The ceiling and gilded trophy panels on the walls are by Joseph Rose. They were inspired by those in the *Villa Madama* in Rome and Adam was so pleased with Rose's work, that it is said he paid for them out of his own pocket. The statuary marble and *verd-antique* chimney piece were carved by Joseph Wilton to designs by Adam. The Wedgwood plaque above is a replica in plaster of an antique relief now in the Louvre, called the *New Bride*.

The two bronze statues are by Valadier. They are of *Silenus with the infant Dionysus* and *Antinous Belvedere*, the favourite of Emperor Hadrian. The gilt tables with marble tops, which came from Rome, are early Adam style. The seat furniture was made in 1823 by Morel and Hughes for Northumberland House.

The architectural interest of the room centres on the clever arrangement of the columns as the room is not really square, but measures 36 feet 6 inches (11.1 metres) by 30 feet (9.1 metres) with a height of 21 feet (6.4 metres). The desired square form is obtained by bringing forward the columns on one side to stand clear of the wall, supporting the entablature which continues around the room. The vertical line is maintained by statues standing upright over the columns. The room thus gives the effect of being square with the minimum loss of floor space.

The right hand window, facing the south lawn, has also been cleverly disguised as a doorway and leads to an external staircase. The hidden door to its right leads to the kitchens and service rooms below stairs. As well as a waiting room the Ante Room would also have been used as a small dining room and King William IV was entertained here in 1832.

Statue of Apollo.

The Dining Room

*The Dining Room was the first of the state rooms to be finished in 1763.
Measuring 66 feet (20.1 metres) by 21 feet 7 inches (6.5 metres),
it is very nearly a triple cube.*

With its arched recesses, apses, half domes and columnar screens, it is quintessentially Adam and illustrative of his declared intention to *'parade the conveniences and the social pleasures of life'*. Adam shows great skill in using screens of Corinthian columns *in antis* before apsidal recesses at each end, thus hiding ugly square corners. The ceiling plaster is the work of Joseph Rose, and the chiaroscuro frieze panels are by Andrea Casali. They depict the mythologies of the *Aldobrandini Wedding*, *The Burning of Meleager's Brand*, and *The Nine Muses*.

The Aldobrandini Wedding by Andrea Casali.

The chimney piece is by Thomas and Benjamin Carter to a design by Adam. Above is a marble panel of the Three Graces, the daughters of Zeus, by Luc-Francois Breton, for which the Duke paid £70.

Joseph Wilton was paid £150 for the copy of Michelangelo's Bacchus, which he made from a cast in the Duke of Richmond's Academy at Whitehall. The statue of *Ceres* is one of the very few complete statues by Bartolomeo Cavaceppi who was known as 'The Prince of Restorers'. The *Apollo* by Francis Harwood was commissioned by James Adam but the Duke was much put out with being provided a blown up copy of a statue famed mainly for its small size! The pier tables are of the early Adam period with the marble tops coming from Italy, the two semi-circular tables by the windows have scagliola tops and all came from Northumberland House.

William Collins' gilt brass lamps, decorated with Percy lions at the base on mahogany pedestals by Morel and Hughes, were made for the Great Dining Room of Northumberland House in 1824.

The clock in the corner of the room is of English manufacture of about 1785 by a renowned Swiss clockmaker, Benjamin Vulliamy. In a gilt metal case, mounted on one side with a Wedgwood medallion and flanked by figures, it is signed on the plinth 'Vulliamy, London'. The pedestal contains musical pipes which play various tunes and is overlaid with scagliola and painted in the centre with an oval monochrome medallion of Apollo driving the chariot of the sun, from a design by Cipriani.

The Red Drawing Room

Adam intended the Red Drawing Room to serve as an Ante Room to the real Withdrawing or Ladies' Room - The Long Gallery. He explained that his reason for making the Gallery the Ladies' Drawing Room was that they should not be disturbed by sounds of revelry emerging from the Dining Room.

The Drawing Room is in vivid contrast to the subtle cream and gold colour scheme of the Dining Room. The wall hangings of crimson Spitalfield silk were probably re-woven in the 1820s and were reversed and re-hung following conservation work carried out in 1965. The coved ceiling, inspired by work in the *Villa Madama*, Rome, was executed by Joseph Rose. The 239 medallions decorating the ceiling are by Cipriani and depict Arcadian figures. They were indirectly referred to by Adam's rival architect, Sir William Chambers, as resembling 'skied dinner plates'. In the 75 central medallions the figures are floating in the heavens, whilst those on the coving around the edge are sitting or standing on solid ground.

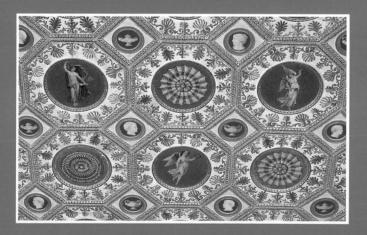

A harewood, burr-yew and marquetry cylinder bureau, c.1780, attributed to Ince and Mayhew.

Thomas Moore, of Moorfields in London, manufactured the carpet in 1769 to a design by Adam. The Greek honeysuckle pattern in the carpet border is repeated around the ceiling medallions, across the fireplace, and on other main features in the room.

The white marble chimney piece is by Thomas and Benjamin Carter to a design by Adam. The doorways are remarkable for the ivory background of the pilaster panels which are filled in with ormolu medallions probably by the founder Diederich Nicolaus Anderson. The gilded lead ornaments were supplied, according to the account books, by Nathaniel Bermingham or Birmingham.

The ormolu used extensively around the doorways and chimney piece is achieved by gilding a metal alloy ~ examples of some of the superb craftsmanship to be found in the Red Drawing Room.

The pier tables in front of the mirrors were designed by Adam and include antique mosaic reputedly from the Baths of Titus in Rome. The mirrors are particularly fine examples of very large sheet glass extending right down to the pier tables and were possibly supplied by the French firm of St. Gobain. The frames were designed by Adam.

The Red Drawing Room during the early part of the 20th century.

The pictures in the room are of the Stuart period and, with the exception of two, depict members of the Royal House of Stuart. The portrait to the left of the Dining Room doorway is of *Elizabeth, Queen of Bohemia* by Van Miereveldt. She was the sister of King Charles I and married King Fredrick V, the Elector Palatine. Known as the "Winter Queen", she was the grandmother of the future King George I of England. Her third son was Prince Rupert, the flamboyant Cavalier soldier. It is interesting to note in the painting the wearing of heirloom jewellery on a piece of black silk string which was the fashion during the early part of the 17th century. It empasised the jewellery and showed up the pale skin of the wearer and the lace of the ruff, as well as possibly preventing over-sized rings from slipping off fingers.

On the other side of the doorway is *Henrietta, Duchess of Orleans*, by Mignard. She was the youngest daughter of King Charles I and known as 'Minette'. She arranged the secret treaty of Dover in 1670 between her brother King Charles II and King Louis XIV of France, but died soon afterwards. The portrait of King Charles II and his wife Queen Catherine of Braganza is attributed to the studio of Lely. King Charles II had no legitimate children and the throne passed on his death in 1685 to his younger brother James, Duke of York. The paintings either side are of King Charles I and James, Duke of York, by Sir Peter Lely. The portrait to the right of the fireplace is thought to be Prince Charles (later King Charles I) or his elder brother Prince Henry who died in 1612, and has been attributed to various artists. The painting of King Charles I and James, Duke of York, by Sir Peter Lely is thought by tradition to have been painted at Syon in 1647. The portrait to its right is painted by a follower of Van Dyck and thought to be Lady Anne Cecil, first wife of the 10th Earl of Northumberland, whose portrait is above the Dining Room doorway. The portrait to the left of the Long Gallery doorway is of Princess Mary of Orange, the first Princess Royal by Adriaen Hanneman. She was the eldest daughter of King Charles I and married William, Prince of Orange. Her son became King William III of England and succeeded King James II in 1689. Above the doorway are the children of King Charles I, after the Van Dyck at Windsor Castle. To the right is a portrait by the studio of Van Dyck of *Henrietta Maria*, wife of King Charles I.

The Long Gallery

The Long Gallery was planned by Adam for the particular delight of the ladies; in his own words 'finished in a style to afford variety and amusement'.

Proposed design for the Long Gallery by Robert Adam

Measuring 136 feet (41.4 metres) by 14 feet (4.2 metres) its length is ten times the width and takes up the whole of the east front, standing over the colonnade. The room is the former Tudor Long Gallery and more than any other reflects the true genius of Adam. He transformed the once panelled gallery by dividing the wall opposite the eleven windows into five bays centred on three doors and two fireplaces, divided by groups of four pilasters comprising book shelves at wide intervals. Originally, alcoves for busts and vases were intended on either side of the doors. By taking the sixty-two Corinthian pilasters, painted by Michelangelo Pergolesi, up to the ceiling he suggested height and by his use of the diagonals in the ceiling he gave an impression of width.

On entering the Gallery from the Red Drawing Room, a false bookcase on the right is in fact a door leading to steps to the south lawn. To the left of the bookcase is one wall panel painted by John Fowler to a colour thought to be close to the original. It was decided not to redecorate the rest of the Gallery, but to leave this as an impression as to how it may have looked. The *stucco duro* roundels are by Joseph Wilton. The carpet incorporates in its borders the original design by Pergolesi of 1765 and was made in 1967 by the Royal Wilton Carpet Company.
The library contains more than 3,000 books.

At each end of the Gallery are small boudoirs or closets known as the turret rooms. The one at the south-east end is square and hung with silk and mirrors painted by the 3rd Duchess and added by Ponsonby. *The Turret Room (opposite)* at the north-east end is exquisitely decorated in rich classical composition stucco, repainted under the direction of John Fowler. Hanging from the domed ceiling is a late 18th century mechanical singing bird with a timepiece.

Much of the furniture, including the window stools, many of the tables and some of the chairs are contemporary with the Adam period *c.* 1765-1775, including the pair of sofas and set of armchairs covered in needlework which came from the Tapestry Room of Northumberland House.

Above the fireplaces are lunettes by Francesco Zuccarelli, a founder member of the Royal Academy. The painted panels of landscapes at each end are by William Marlow. The portrait medallions around the Gallery show the lineage of the Percy family, which claims descent from Charlemagne, the first Emperor of the Holy Roman Empire. The portraits up to, and possibly including, that of the 2nd Duke are by Francis Lindo, a local Isleworth artist. The medallion opposite the second fireplace is of Harry Hotspur.

The Nautilus Shell is a 19th century copy of the 16th century original in Windsor Castle, made by the German goldsmith, Nicholas Schmidt of Nuremberg.

Looking out of the Gallery windows at the views across the tidal water meadows of the River Thames towards Kew Gardens, it is hard to imagine that one is only a few miles from central London. The meadows are registered as a Site of Special Scientific Interest and are separated by a ha-ha, an 18th century landscape feature devised to prevent livestock encroaching onto the formal parkland. In the distance to the left can be seen a small fence surrounding a mulberry tree, one of a number of trees that are thought to date back to the 17th century.

The Print Room

In 1824 the 3rd Duke paid Thomas Ponsonby and his men to remove one hundred prints and their borders from the walls, but the room has retained its name until the present day. The 1st Duchess of Northumberland was a great collector of prints which she bought in large quantities while travelling on the Continent.

The Print Room forms part of the alterations along the north side of the house, made by the 3rd Duke. The ceiling was executed during the reign of his brother, the 4th Duke by Charles Smith to a design by Montiroli in 1863~4. Portraits of many of the people who made the history of Syon hang in this room. Amongst them are the *Protector Somerset, Somerset's two wives* and his son *Edward Seymour, Earl of Hertford.* The portrait of *Lady Jane Grey* is also thought to be *Princess (later Queen) Elizabeth.* Family portraits include the *9th Earl of Northumberland (the 'Wizard' Earl)* by Thomas Phillips, after Van Dyck, and the *10th Earl of Northumberland,* by Sir Peter Lely, after Van Dyck. There are two portraits of *Lady Elizabeth Percy,* afterwards Duchess of Somerset, by Sir Peter Lely, as well as the *Earl and Countess of Hertford* and their daughter *Elizabeth, later 1st Duchess of Northumberland.* There are also portraits of the *1st Duke of Northumberland* by Gainsborough, the *1st Duchess of Northumberland,* by Sir Joshua Reynolds and the *2nd Duke of Northumberland* by the 18th century North American portrait painter Gilbert Stuart.

Three portraits in this room have particularly interesting North American links. *Major John Norton,* painted by Thomas Phillips, was a British officer who lived with the Native Americans, marrying a local woman. He was known as Chief Teyoninhokarawen and his *'Journey of 1,000 miles down the Ohio',* written in 1809, was dedicated to Hugh, 2nd Duke of Northumberland, who fought in the American War of Independence.

George Percy - note a finger is missing on his left hand, which he lost fighting in one of his campaigns.

George Percy (1580-1632), the 9th Earl's younger brother, accompanied Sir Walter Raleigh to America. Later he became the Acting Governor of Jamestown, Virginia in 1611.

A further connection between the Percy family and America concerns *James Smithson* (1765-1829), the natural son of the 1st Duke of Northumberland and Elizabeth Macie. He was a member of the Royal Society and his will stated that in the absence of descendants, his money should be left to '*The United States of America, to found at Washington, under the name of the Smithsonian Institute, an establishment for the increase and diffusion of knowledge among men*'. The bequest was paid in gold sovereigns and delivered to the United States mint at Philadelphia, where it was valued in excess of half a million dollars.

Joseph Brant

Hugh Smithson, 1st Duke of Northumberland by Thomas Gainsborough.

Joseph Brant (1742-1807) painted by Gilbert Stuart, was a celebrated Indian chieftain of the Mohawk tribe and head of Iroquois Confederacy in the State of New York. His Mohawk name was Thayandanegea and he was of mixed blood. He rendered valuable assistance to the British during the American War, and later visited England including Syon House. Given an opportunity to kiss the King's hand, he compromised and offered to kiss the Queen's hand. He too was associated in America with the 2nd Duke of Northumberland, and Brantford, Ontario, is named in his honour.

The two ebony and "pietra dura" cabinets are of 17th century origin. They were originally in Northumberland House and their stands were made in 1825 by Morel and Hughes, as was the circular rosewood table, housing the mosaic top by Rafaelli representing Bacchus.

The Duchess' Sitting Room

Although much altered, this room forms part of the inner suite of family rooms dating back to the 16th century and is shown on Robert Adam's plan of the house as a bedchamber. More recently it has been used as a family sitting room.

The attractive marble fireplace, with its carved plaque representing Aesop's *Fable of the Fox and the Stork*, was brought from Northumberland House. The two 18th century armchairs in front of it have tapestry covers stitched by Helen, 8th Duchess, and her sister in the 1930s. Other 18th century pieces here include the bow-front satinwood commode and the mahogany display cabinet by Vile, both against the wall to the left, and the Queen Anne walnut bureau cabinet on the right. The concertina-action George II card table, on which the chess set is displayed,

is one of a pair and the unusual two-tier table was originally two stools and is also part of a set. This dates from the early 19th century, as does the impressive calamander wood library writing table in the centre of the room. Both were made by Morel and Hughes for Northumberland House

Much of the porcelain is 18th century, both European and Oriental, and the paintings are mainly Dutch, collected by the 1st Duchess.

The Green Drawing Room

The Green Drawing Room is still regularly used by the family.
The ornate Renaissance-style ceiling, as in the Print Room and Dining Room,
was designed by Giovanni Montiroli and executed by Charles Smith in 1863~4.

The superb scagliola fireplace, designed by Adam for the Glass Drawing Room of Northumberland House, was installed in 1924. The grate is made of paktong, an alloy of copper, nickel and zinc smelted originally by the Chinese which does not tarnish. Much of the furniture is 18th century, including the suite of beechwood seat furniture, the two marquetry serpentine commodes standing either side of the fireplace, and the Italian topped micro-mosaic giltwood side tables on the left hand side of the room. The chandelier is English and dates from the 1830s.

Many of the paintings are 17th and 18th century portraits of royalty and members of the Percy family. Those of particular interest include the portraits of *King Edward VI* as an infant, attributed to a follower of Holbein, above the fireplace. The two portraits by Van Dyck hang either side: *Frances Devereux* (left) and *Mrs Endymion Porter* (right). *Albrecht Dürer's father* by Richard Greenbury, after Dürer, is below the Porter portrait and *Andrew Drummond* by Sir Joshua Reynolds is above the piano.

The Private Dining Room

This room has been used as a private dining room since Robert Adam remodelled the house.

The spectacular gilt-brass waterfall chandelier made by William Collins dates from about 1825 and was made for the Glass Drawing Room of Northumberland House. It is designed as a fountain, with three entwined dolphins spouting jets of water and hung with glass beads depicting droplets of water.

Much of the furniture here dates from the early 19th century and was supplied for this room by Robert Hughes. This includes the mahogany extending table, the dining chairs, the two large sideboards with cellarets or wine coolers and the two marble-topped tables. Dating from about 1770 are the two mahogany pedestals, each with a lidded leaf carved cistern and a cupboard below, standing at each end of the sideboard at the far end of the room.

Displayed on the sideboards and table are pieces of richly gilded French porcelain from the Paris Dagoty dessert service, purchased by the 3rd Duke in the 1820s.

Outstanding among the portraits are those of the 1st Duke, by James Barry, and his Duchess, after Sir Joshua Reynolds, over the sideboards. The charming family group of the *2nd Duke's children*, painted by Gilbert Stuart at Syon in the summer of 1787 hangs above the fireplace.

The Oak Passage

The passage is another of the 3rd Duke's additions made during the 1820s to provide a service corridor. Today it contains many interesting royal and family portraits. The wall to the left is part of the outer wall of the original house.

The wainscot panelling probably dates from the early 16th century and it is thought that these panels came from Leconfield, a former Percy residence in Yorkshire, and were brought to Syon by the 9th Earl. They may have originally been painted in the Percy colours of blue and gold (top right). The chairs were made for the waiting hall of Northumberland House by Morel and Hughes in 1823. The map dated 1635 by Moses Glover of the "*Istelworth Hundred*" and the "*Mannor at Sion*", and the copy of Jan Griffier's painting of Syon and its surroundings are of particular interest.

The wainscot panelling, digitally altered to show how it may have looked in the early 16th century.

Prince Arthur, elder brother of Henry VIII.

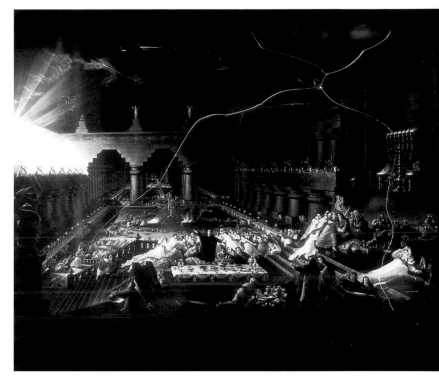

'Belshazzar's Feast' by John 'Mad' Martin (1789-1854). Martin painted this copy of his original on glass so that if lit from behind, it could be displayed in a window. This was done in order to advertise the display of the original inside the building.

A copy of Canaletto's painting of Syon in 1749 (now on display at Alnwick Castle). Sir Hugh Smithson (later the 1st Duke) recorded 'Mr Canaletti has begun the picture of Syon and by the outlines upon the canvas I think it will have a noble effect'.

Northumberland House

The use of Northumberland House, the family's principal London residence, and of Syon was very much linked. Built in 1605 for the Earl of Northampton, the house came to the Percy family in 1642 on the 10th Earl of Northumberland's marriage to Elizabeth Howard, daughter of the Earl of Suffolk, and was renamed Northumberland House. The house had 150 private rooms for the family as well as the usual offices and service rooms and extended from the Strand to the river. When demolished by the Metropolitan Board of Works in 1874, Northumberland House was the last of London's great private riverside palaces.

Canaletto's painting of Northumberland House (now on display at Alnwick Castle), clearly shows the statant lion, after a model by Michelangelo, which was removed to Syon where it can be seen today on the east front of the house.

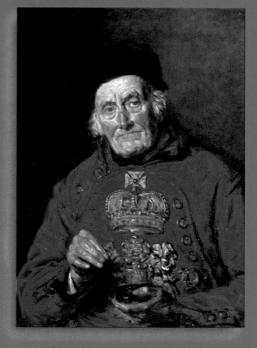

William Timms was 95 years old in 1838 when this portrait was painted by Emma Soyer. He served three sovereigns and three Dukes of Northumberland as waterman.

Robert Adam was commissioned by the 1st Duke to undertake work on one of his most spectacular creations in the design of the Glass Drawing Room. A small section of the Drawing Room has been reconstructed in the British Galleries at the Victoria and Albert Museum. Some of the furniture from the house, including fireplaces and the chandelier from the Glass Drawing Room are now at Syon.

The oar near the portrait of William Timms is from the Duke's state barge. The River Thames was a principal thoroughfare for noblemen travelling to and from their houses or attending court and the 1st Duke and Duchess would journey between Northumberland House and Syon for an evening's entertainment. The impressive colonnaded east front of the house as seen in Canaletto's painting could be admired by passing traffic on the river.

The Principal Staircase

Leading off the West Corridor is the principal staircase. In the well can be seen the Sèvres vase given by the French King Charles X to the 3rd Duke, who attended his coronation in 1825 as Great Britain's Ambassador Extraordinary.

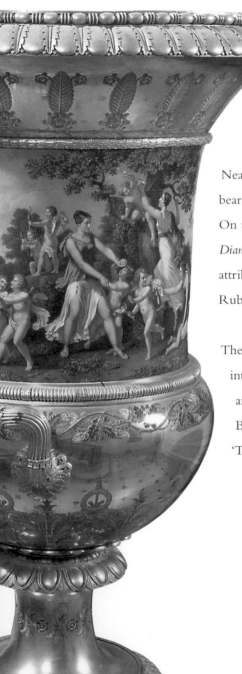

Near the vase is a sedan chair, bearing the arms of the 1st Duke. On the wall is the painting *Diana returning from the Hunt*, attributed to the studio of Rubens and de Vos.

The West Corridor leads back into the Great Hall, and so ends what Sir John Betjeman described as 'The Grand Architectural Walk'.

'Diana returning from the Hunt' attributed to the studio of Rubens and de Vos.

The Duchess of Kent's Bedroom.

The Upper Floor

This part of the house is still in private use. An inventory carried out in 1847 at the time of the 3rd Duke's death gives a detailed description of every room in the house and the present-day layout reflects the remodelling undertaken during the 1820s and 1830s.

The main staircase leads to the landing along the North Front or the Nursery Passage. The two bedrooms on view here were described in 1847 as the Pink and Blue bedrooms, with their adjoining dressing rooms. They have been furnished in a turn of the century style. The present Duke, with his brothers and sisters, occupied these rooms as children when the family visited Syon each year during the late spring and early summer. The first (Pink) bedroom was their nursery dayroom.

Bedrooms along the Nursery Passage.

The East Front

This wing contains the principal suite of State bedrooms, furnished by Robert Hughes in 1832 for the use of the young Princess Victoria (below), and her mother, the Duchess of Kent.

Queen Victoria in 1838, painted one year after she ascended the throne, by the American, Thomas Sully.
Reproduced by permission of the Trustees of the Wallace Collection, London.

The giltwood four poster bed in the Duchess of Kent's room dates from 1790 but was substantially altered by Hughes, who added a footboard, new cornices and tester together with hangings of '*blue silk taberet*'. He also supplied a new '*Polonese Bedstead*' for the Princess in her bedroom (*opposite*). The same blue silk taberet was used for the hangings embellished with the half circle gold gimp and restrained by tassels at each corner. Each bed had three mattresses: the lower one of straw, the second of horsehair or wool, and the top layer, known as the bed rather than a mattress, filled with chicken or goose feathers. Hughes also supplied a feather bolster and two down pillows, three '*superfine*' Witney blankets and a Marseilles quilt for each bed.

The Household and Entertaining

Syon has throughout the centuries hosted some lavish parties since the 9th Earl entertained King James I in 1603. This banquet cost the equivalent of £20,000 in today's money, of which more than £6,000 was spent on wine. The family and household consumed enormous amounts of food and drink. In the 10th Earl's time, for example, an annual account records that 200 barrels of beer, 4,197 dozen loaves and 18 cakes, plus a parmesan wedge weighing 35 lbs were purchased for his lordship's table.

In the mid-18th century the 1st Duchess employed 50 servants and was keen to practise economy in her household. She made the calculation that a servant would eat a pound of meat, half a pound of potatoes, a loaf of bread and two pints of beer a day, at a total cost of no more than 8 pence each. She was also very particular in the way she expected the servants to behave when at Syon and she drew up a set of rules for the Servants' Hall.

THE DAILY ROUTINE AND RULES FOR THE SERVANTS,
WRITTEN BY THE 1ST DUCHCESS.

HOURS TO BE OBSERVED

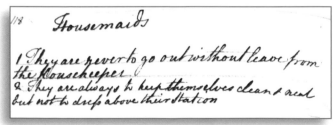

HOUSEMAIDS

SERVANTS' HALL

At the beginning of the 19th century, a detailed set of 'Regulations' replaced these rules. The 2nd Duke, a military man, liked to order his household as if he were in command of a regiment, and a clear distinction was drawn between the upper-servants and those who performed the more mundane duties.

The upper-servants included the Steward of the Household, the Valet de Chambre, the Groom of the Chambers and the Butler – each of whom had specific duties in the smooth running of the household. This was under the overall control of the Steward while the Groom looked after the apartments and saw to it that the servants were well turned out; the Valet's duties were personal to the family and the Butler had charge of the silverware and the wine cellar.

The Duke demanded the very highest service and exemplary behaviour from his upper-servants expecting them to be a shining example to those whom they controlled. He regarded the whole household of servants as part of the 'family' for whom he was personally responsible and a servant could only be dismissed from the household on his personal command.

Much of the economy of the household, as well as the social prestige of the family, rested on the kitchen, where there were three principal servants - the Clerk of the Kitchen who ordered the food supplies, the Cook who created the menu and oversaw the daily working of the kitchen and the Confectioner, who was the specialist purveyor of the sorbets, ices and jellies which graced the tables when the Duke and Duchess entertained. According to the figures given in the Clerk of Kitchen's lists in the first fortnight in August 1820, the household consumed 578lbs of beef, 225lbs of mutton and 144lbs of veal as well as 25 head of poultry and rabbits. In addition 260 eggs and 31lbs of butter together with 3 pecks of flour, 52 loaves and 7^1/$_4$lbs of tea were provided.

An inventory of the house at the time of the 3rd Duke's death in 1847 provides a full description of the basement of the house. The basement contained staff quarters, including the Steward's Room and the Servants' Hall, the former providing for the upper servants, while the latter catered for the lower.

The Confectionery was a major department of the household and the Confectioner had his own bedroom, complete with chintz curtains, Brussels carpet, bed with hair mattress and a mahogany table. The Confectioner also

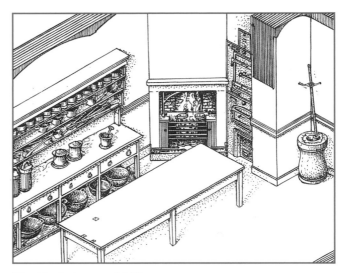

The Confectionery c.1830.   P.Brears

had his own cellar below stairs, with preserving pans, stewing stoves, sieves and steamers and 10 pewter freezing pots. The bedrooms of the Clerk of the Kitchens and the Cook were attached to the kitchen area on the north side of the house. The kitchen itself contained a range, spits, stewing stoves and a whole range of copper and tin equipment including 83 stew pans, coppers for baking, sauce pans, small kettles and a fish kettle large enough to take a turbot.

The basement also contained the Secretary's room, the Housekeeper's room and the Valet de Chambre's bedroom, together with the sleeping quarters for eight footman and male servants; while the laundry maids had their own quarters alongside the laundry and wash house. The postillions and coachmen were housed in the stable block along with the Master of Horse. There was also a separate sick bay for servants who fell ill.

These cut-away drawings by Peter Brears are conjectural and are based on inventories taken in 1632 and 1847.

The house depicted at the time of the 9th Earl's death.
The principal room on the west front was the Hall. The Long Gallery as today, ran the length of the east front. The south front contained the Dining Room, the Withdrawing Chamber and three bedrooms. The attached brick building on the north side housed the kitchen range and the corresponding building on the south side, lodgings.

The house depicted at the time of the 3rd Duke's death.
The rooms on the principal floor follow a similar layout as today. The main difference is the kitchen range to the north which is now garages and staff accommodation.

The basement contained, staff quarters and service areas.
The vaulted undercroft below the Great Hall was used as the Confectioner's cellar; the Confectionery, located below the Ante Room faced south to catch the best light. The Butler's plate pantry and servants' bedrooms occupied the remainder of the south front. Further servants' bedrooms were on the east side of the house behind the colonnade. The Steward's Room and Servant's Hall were on the north side, with the Housekeeper's room situated at the end of the passage facing west.

SYON PARK as in 1632
P. Brears delt. MMI

SYON PARK
The London Home of the Dukes of Northumberland, as in 1847
P. Brears delt. MMI

SYON PARK
The London Home of the Dukes of Northumberland
THE BASEMENT as in 1847
P. Brears delt. MMI

Annual Wages in 1845:

Cook (Louis Limousin) £150
Confectioner £110
Footmen £28
Laundry Maids £14
Total Salary Bill £753

Throughout the Victorian era and much of the 20th
century, Syon was used as a summer residence by the
family, and the Royal Family and other distinguished guests
were often entertained.

*'More than one hundred tenants sat down
to dinner in the Great Hall. The delicacies
of the season and rare wines from the old
cellars of the Mansion heightened the
enjoyment of the feast which was furnished
with the traditional Barons of Beef, and the
Band of the Grenadier Guards gave the
company some delightful music'.*

Account of a banquet given
by the 5th Duke in 1867

SYON.

PÉJEUNER DU 15 JUILLET, 1886.

MENU.

Pâté chaud froid de Cailles.
Galantine de Volaille.
Jambon à l'Aspic.
Bœuf à l'Ecarlate.
Petits Aspics à la Cardinal.
Profitrolles à l'Indienne.
Profitrolles à la Reine.
Chaud froid de Volaille.
Chaud froid de Cailles Truffés.
Poulets rôtis.
Jambon.
Langue de Bœuf.
Sandwiches—Volaille, Jambon, Langue, Strasbourg.
Babas.
Gelées.
Crêmes.
Macedoine de Fruits.
Pâtisseries.
Gateaux.

A 19th century menu from one of Syon House's banquets.

A Victorian garden party at Syon.

The Gardens

The gardens at Syon Park contain elements from several historic periods but are continually changing, both over the years and through the seasons.

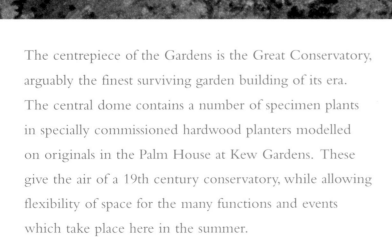

The centrepiece of the Gardens is the Great Conservatory, arguably the finest surviving garden building of its era. The central dome contains a number of specimen plants in specially commissioned hardwood planters modelled on originals in the Palm House at Kew Gardens. These give the air of a 19th century conservatory, while allowing flexibility of space for the many functions and events which take place here in the summer.

The wings are planted with a collection of shrubs and flowers to give an exotic effect, and lead to two small pavilions containing cacti and ferns respectively. While the Great Conservatory is now completely unheated throughout the year, it does provide some degree of protection which enables the cultivation of less hardy plants.

Beyond the Great Conservatory, lies the lake. It was 'Capability' Brown's intention that this should appear to be a completely natural stretch of water, and it forms the centrepiece of the Pleasure Grounds. The lake is about a quarter of a mile in length, and holds a wide variety of fish as well as providing a home for waterfowl.

The walk alongside the lake takes the visitor past some of Syon's finest trees, but it is worth leaving the lakeside to visit the Woodland Garden, where camellias and rhododendrons are underplanted with bulbs and a collection of herbaceous woodland plants. Most woodland plants flower before the leaf canopy overhead has become too dense, and so this area is at its best in spring and early summer.

Beyond the woodland area is Flora's Lawn, dominated by a statue of *Flora, Goddess of flowers,* atop a 55ft doric column. While the column has stood since the mid-18th century, the original statue of Flora was struck by lightning in the 1970s, and the current statue is a replica.

Opposite Flora is one of the finest trees at Syon, a magnificent Caucasian elm, *Zelkova carpinifolia,* beneath which is a gravel garden with a collection of drought resistant herbaceous plants.

Another area of arboretum lies beyond *Flora's Column,* and several areas of wildflowers have been established here. Near the lake there is a spring meadow, where cowslips and primroses are mingled with lady's smock and ragged robin in March and April.

The banks around the far end of the lake were built up to prevent the regular tidal flooding which previously occurred, and the resulting poor soil provides suitable conditions for a variety of wildflowers, including orchids, ox-eye daisies, and vetches. This area is at its best in midsummer, when it is full of butterflies and other insects.

The path then leads through the Duke's private woodland, which contains more fine specimen trees, including some of the largest swamp cypresses, *Taxodium distichum,* in the country. A characteristic of these trees is their habit of sending up pneumatophores, which allow roots to breathe in their native Mississippi swamps. Some of these stilt roots stand more than a metre high, which is unique in Britain. These woods are full of daffodils and bluebells in the spring, while in the winter there are views across the Tide Meadow towards the east front of Syon House.

To the south of Syon House can be found the Rose Garden and Wilderness. This area was the site of the earliest gardens at Syon, but the only visible evidence of these early gardens is to be seen where the boundary of the Rose Garden looks towards the south front of Syon House, where the hollow matches the location of the 10th Earl's Great Fountain, celebrated by John Evelyn in the 17th century. In the late 18th century these grounds were swept away to create a wilderness dominated by the new plants just arriving from North America, and this is reflected to in the American Border, planted with shrubs of the period.

The Rose Garden Square itself was originally laid out in the 1960s, but restored and replanted within the last ten years. It holds a collection of more than 100 different varieties of old fashioned shrub roses, including gallicas, rugosas, floribunda and damask roses. A number of climbing roses are trained onto pillars, and the main flowering is in midsummer, with a second flush in the autumn.

Beyond the square, open lawns with fine specimen trees run to the south. The ha-ha runs along the east of this area, and superbly serves its function as a concealed barrier to the cattle grazing in tide meadow. There are views across the meadow to King George III's Royal Observatory in the Richmond Old Deer Park, and along the Syon Vista to the Palm House in Kew Gardens. Beyond a magnificent spreading cedar, *Cedrus libani*, a raised viewpoint allows the visitor to look over the wall towards the parkland and the Outer Lake.

Courtesy of
The Royal
Horticultural
Society.

The Parkland and Ecology

The fields and parkland surrounding Syon House cover around 50 hectares, and are of considerable importance in their own right. Although long since surrounded by the spread of London, the park preserves a rural quality and is a haven for a wide variety of wildlife.

The Canaletto landscape of the mid-18th century shows cattle grazing in the fields around Syon House, and the fields at Syon are still grazed today.

Large areas of the park have been managed in the same way for generations, and this continuity is central to the ecology of the estate. The most striking example is the front lawn, to the west of Syon House, which has always provided the formal approach to Syon House, and is likely to have been

kept as some form of lawn or mown grass since the 15th century. This continuity has lead to a distinctive community of plants and fungi, some extremely rare, the lawn effectively forming a historical artefact older than the house.

The antiquity of the buildings and landscape have allowed a remarkable number of fungi to flourish, with more than 140 species recorded, as well as more than 50 species of

lichen. The ecological richness of particular locations can also provide evidence as to their history as a high count of species can indicate an area which has lain undisturbed for centuries.

Although the parkland was landscaped by 'Capability' Brown in the mid-18th century, it was his practice to preserve features from older landscapes, and several trees date from a time when this area was fields and farmland. Britain has the best population of ancient trees in the world, many of which have great importance for associated plants and animals, especially insects, birds and bats. The older trees at Syon are valued for the central place they play in the parkland ecosystem, and the habitats they provide, as well as for their antiquity. Syon has a good population of bats, and it is likely that this is in part due to the roosts available in the decay pockets and broken branches of ancient trees.

Quércus rùbra.
The red-leaved, or Champion, Oak.

From a full-grown tree at Syon, 57 ft. high; diam. of the head, 55 ft.
[Scale 1 in. to 12 ft.]

Courtesy of
The Royal
Horticultural
Society.

Grasslands are important for the conservation not only of plants, but also of other species, notably invertebrates. The Duchess' Meadow to the east of Syon House is alive with butterflies and other insects in the summer, and care is taken to promote these species, by encouraging nectar-rich plants and leaving areas uncut. The presence of the insects attracts those species that feed upon them, and the meadows are popular with ground-nesting birds such as pheasants. Smaller birds appreciate the shelter and diversity of the gardens, and these in turn attract the attentions of the resident birds of prey.

Gardens comprise one of the most ecologically important habitats in Britain, as the diversity of species leads to a variety of sources of food and shelter, encouraging a wide range of insects, birds and mammals. At Syon, around 200 different trees species and many more shrubs and flowers mean that there is shelter and food over much of the year, with no shortage of nesting sites. Syon is fortunate in its proximity to the Thames and for having a long and sheltered lake, containing good numbers of fish which in turn attract grey herons and cormorants. More exotic inhabitants include a pair of Egyptian geese who visit the park

annually, red-eared terrapins, and ring-necked parakeets: unmistakable, vivid green birds, swooping through the trees in noisy flocks.

The most important ecological site on the estate is the tide meadow, an area of tidal grassland containing the only significant stretch of natural river bank remaining on the tidal Thames. This unique quality has lead to the tide meadow being classified as a Site of Special Scientific Interest, the only such site on the tidal river. Large parts of the meadow are flooded twice a day at high tide, and while relatively dry near the ha-ha, it becomes wetter towards the river, where it is intersected by a network of pools, creeks and gullies. The Thames is one of the cleanest metropolitan rivers in the world, supporting more than 130 species of fish and 350 species of invertebrates, and an important

© The Natural History Museum, London

breeding site for North Sea fish, ranging from sea bass to plaice; these creeks provide excellent feeding and refuge areas for young fish. The tide meadow is also notable as one of the few habitats of the rare

German hairy snail (*Perforatella rubiginosa*).

The creeks and the tidal nature of the meadow make it unsafe for visitors and there is no direct public access, but there are good views from the platform in the Duke's Woodland and from the ha-ha in the Rose Garden.

Although the tide meadow was planted with clumps of trees in the 18th and 19th centuries, the continuous belt of trees along the riverside is relatively modern, having largely colonised over the last 50 years. In recent years a series of vistas have been cut through this belt of trees to allow views through to the river and to Kew Gardens and the Royal Observatory. This is part of the *Thames Landscape Strategy*, an initiative formed to raise appreciation of the riverside landscape.

Courtesy of
The Royal
Horticultural
Society.

Full-grown tree at Syon, 63 ft. high.
[Scale 1 in. to 12 ft.]

Harvest time during the First World War.

The Home Farm & Dairy House

There was a working farm within Syon Park until the farm buildings were converted for the Gardening Centre in the 1960s. The first farm at Syon would have been established by the Bridgettines for the abbey. It is probable that a section of walling in the much altered monastery barn in the Garden Centre may date from the 16th century.

During the reign of the 2nd Duke farming became an integral part of Syon activity. The farm was intended to serve the economy of the ducal household at both Syon and Northumberland House.

HM Queen Elizabeth the Queen Mother, who opened the Garden Centre on the 12th June 1968.

The monastery barn at the beginning of the 20th century.

The 4th Duke had a herd of two dozen Jersey cattle brought from his Stanwick estate. He also added a herd of *Highland cattle* to add a romantic look to the park.

Pigs were kept to fatten on the dairy's whey. By the second half of the 19th century a flock of Southdown sheep grazed the parkland. Hounslow fair was a popular market for sales. The livestock provided the conservatory and gardens with a plentiful supply of manure, and the new visitor centre was the slaughter yard!

An ice house was in use at Syon by 1760-1761, when it is recorded it took twelve men two days to fill it with ice from the lake.

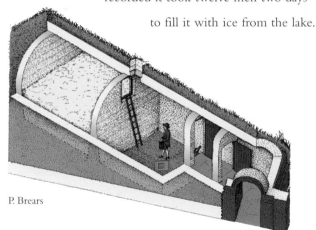

P. Brears

A new ice-house,

between the house and the Great Conservatory, was built during the 1820s with two connecting chambers, where ice could survive through the summer months. The ice was used by the Confectioner whose chief duty was to provide the Duke's table with

ice cream, sorbets or cool drinks. A dairy house built in 1797-1799, provided a full range of practical facilities, including lodgings for the dairy maid. After the accession of the 4th Duke, in 1847, it was extended by building the present dairy, attributed to a design by Decimus Burton. Every detail was carefully planned with marble benches, shelves and balustrades, and a fine floor of colourful encaustic tiles. The Duke and his guests could enjoy visits to this elegant dairy, entering it from the Great Conservatory, while the dairy maid continued to carry out most of the practical work in the older dairy nearby.

One of the four plaster panels by Joseph Gott, in the dairy house.

The four plaster panels set into the walls of the dairy show infant boys (*putti*) milking goats, racing greyhounds and harvesting grapes. The 4th Duke commissioned them from Joseph Gott (1786-1860), a leading portrait and animal sculptor who had worked in Rome since 1822. With their playful figures, imaginative design and skilful modelling, they represent some of his finest work.

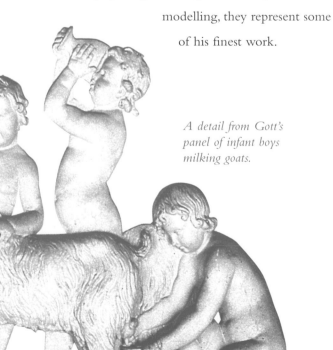

A detail from Gott's panel of infant boys milking goats.

Hospitality and Events at Syon Park

'So as to accommodate to the manners of different nations' was one of the key aims of Robert Adam, when remodelling the interior of Syon House for the 1st Duke of Northumberland.

This desire to fashionably entertain guests on a lavish scale is as relevant today as it was in the 1760s, and Syon House continues to host both corporate and private events including dinners, meetings, promotions, lectures and concerts for clients from many countries. The Great Hall of Syon House is licensed for civil wedding ceremonies, while wedding receptions and private parties are held from spring to autumn in the Great Conservatory. Marquees in the parkland, make an idyllic 'rural' setting for larger corporate and private functions such as fashion shows, film premières, balls, dinner dances and conferences. One of the most recent prestigious events, was the Versace/De Beers Millennium celebration, *The Diamonds are Forever* Charity Fashion Show, attended by HRH The Prince of Wales and celebrities from across the world.

Naomi Campbell poses at the Versace Party, in front of HRH The Prince of Wales and to his right Catherine Zeta Jones.

Photo Rooke/Rex Features

Light Bitz

Syon Park in Films

Syon Park's unique historic buildings and landscaped parkland on the river Thames, so close to London and major studios, makes it a favourite location for feature films and television productions, as well as magazine and newspaper photography shoots.

Henry, 11th Duke of Northumberland (1988-1995) had a passion for film-making and owned a production company, *Hotspur Productions*. His company was associated in the making of the feature film *Lost in Africa* and *Harry Percy* (as he appears on the credits) played the part of George.

Feature films using Syon Park as a location include: *THE MADNESS OF KING GEORGE*, starring Sir Nigel Hawthorne, Helen Mirren, Ian Holm, Rupert Everett and Rupert Graves; *THE WINGS OF THE DOVE*, with Helena Bonham Carter, Linus Roache, Michael Gambon and Charlotte Rampling. *THE AVENGERS* with Sean Connery, Ralph Fiennes and Uma Thurman, and Merchant Ivory's *THE GOLDEN BOWL*, starring Nick Nolte, Uma Thurman, James Fox, Anjelica Huston, Jeremy Northam and Kate Beckinsale.

© Buena Vista

Kate Beckinsale in The Golden Bowl.

The acclaimed *GOSFORD PARK* was shot at Syon House in April 2001. The Director, Robert Altman, particularly admired the bedrooms and in the film these became Sir William McCordle's (Michael Gambon) family and guests' bedrooms. The memorable scenes of '*the date with hot milk*' between Lady Sylvia (Kristin Scott Thomas) and Mr Weissman's valet, Henry Denton, (Ryan Phillippe), were shot in one of the nursery wing bedrooms. Meanwhile, the nursery wing corridor acted as an upstairs thoroughfare for the servants, particularly Robert Parks, Probert, George and Elsie, played by Clive Owen, Derek Jacobi, Richard E Grant and Emily Watson.

The People's Duchess

© Stuart Chorley

Notable television productions have included *THE PEOPLE'S DUCHESS* and *LONGITUDE* on Channel 4, *WIVES AND DAUGHTERS, LOVE IN A COLD CLIMATE, DANIEL DERONDA, THE LOST PRINCE* and *THE ANTIQUES ROADSHOW* on BBC1.

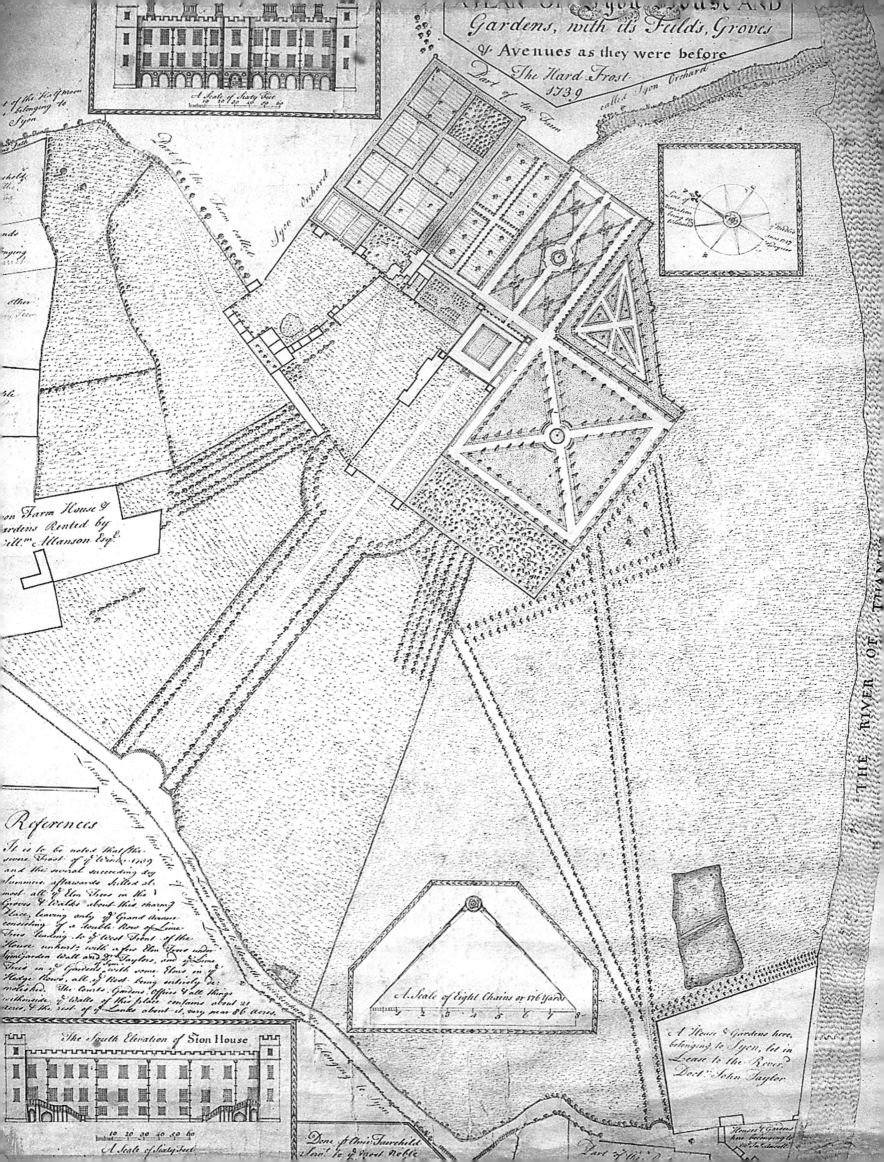

A PLAN of Syon House AND
Gardens, with its Feilds, Groves
& Avenues as they were before
The Hard Frost
1739

Part of the Town called Syon Orchard

A Scale of Sixty Feet
10 20 30 40 50 60

References

The South Elevation of Sion House

10 20 30 40 50 60
A Scale of Sixty feet

A Scale of Eight Chains or 176 yards
1 2 3 4 5 6 7 8

THE RIVER OF THAMES

A House & Gardens here,
belonging to Syon, let in
Lease to the River
Doctr John Taylor